On the evening of the eighth day
God said, Everyone's a critic.
This cannot end well.
                    —*Apocryphal*

3201 e's

Kevin J Taylor

"Perhaps where life has paused
Or slowed enough to perceive
At any speed
The speed of perception
The true speed of light
The wavelengths of laughter
And of any thing"

Finding Buddha,
a hymn in 4 poems

ISBN: 9781983359835
Imprint: Independently published

Self published writings— tales, poems and thoughts which have occupied my mind.

Some of these pieces have previously seen the light of day in earlier forms. The stories are very short— a carry-over from decades of writing verse. These pages offer physical form to the intangible. They are portals between us.

poetkevinjtaylor@gmail.com

Kevin J Taylor, poet
308-13226 104 Avenue
Surrey, British Columbia
CANADA V3T 1V1

Contents

Head bowed

You sit

Let us say

Cataclysm

The Mathematics of the Shattered Soul

Enjoy the sunshine when she comes

One Cat, Maybe Two

The New Apartheid

Paris, 13 November

Them Birds That Cat

For I do love

Softly

WAR

Are we beggars

clatter fades

At least until this fairy tale is over

Embittered Immortal

Hymn of the Fallen Tree

Not much to tell

Still here, my friend, not much to tell.
Winter came, wearied, went.
Spring— hurried skies, or sun or rain.
Hot summer days, hot sleepless nights.
Fall was fresher, raked what fell.
Another year. Mostly well.

We Have Gone On (9/11)

Take away the sun above
> *Take away the sun above,*

And burn the air we breathe.
> *Burn the air we breathe.*

Take away the moon, the stars
> *The moon, the stars.*

And everything believed.
> *Everything believed.*

Take away the green of life—
> *Green of life.*

The blue-green seas below
> *The seas below.*

And take the glow that lives in them
> *Take the glow that lives in them.*

And everything unknown.
> *All things unknown.*

Take the candle. Take the verse.
> *Take the candle. Take the verse.*

Take art and take the artist's words.
> *The artist's words.*

Take each thing— its form, its name.
> *Form and name.*

Take everything. What's left to say?
> *Everything. Everything.*

One thing's for sure— We have survived.

Here we are.
One thing's for sure— We will survive!
We carry on. Carry on.
We have gone on and left this song behind.

I don't care

I don't care who your god is
    It's alright who your god is
I don't care how you pray
    It's alright
All I care is where my heart is—
    Here. Here my heart is
What I do with it today

The Hateful Man

Let each hate, and ours for his,
Be scraped away. Hopefully,
He cared for some, at least the few
That may have cared for him.

Allow unchanged what good remains.
At length, with love or hate or both,
We go. In time, some with pause
and some without, return.

Everybody's Man

I have not come, he says,
to defend God,
but to offend sinners.

> Looks straight at me—
> I am everybody's man.

If Love Exists

Love early, long and more than any heart can hold,
full souled! First, last and freshly found. Love in all.
Love all in all. By these words, if love exists, love all.

If (when)

If, for example, we die (and I've heard otherwise).
Not if but when, I've heard.
I would argue (suggest)
There is no truer when than now.
We live unless (until) we say we die.

And only then, if I agree
And we agree
And others too
And once agreed
Must not be spoken of

(Which, all said, appears
To be the dyingness).

Contrariwise,
Living, living now and thus—
If (when) we'll agree amongst ourselves—
L'chaim!

Finding Buddha, a hymn in 4 poems

The first poem takes place during the lifetime of Lord Buddha. The second poem follows in the years soon after Lord Buddha left his body. The third poem is the mind of the boy (the spirit of the boy in the first poem) in restless meditation. He has yet to attain full enlightenment. There are other voices suggested by parentheses and which are whispered words. If you prefer linear thought or literal interpretation this poem may not communicate to you. Just as a painting may be abstract, this poem is wide open to your own connections, thoughts and emotions. If you like, you can skip to the fourth poem. The fourth poem in three lines lies within this portion of eternity that is forever present time.

Boy runner (the first poem)

Approaching Gautama where He sat a
boy examined Him politely. (This-that?)
Gautama spoke and there the unnamed boy,
who sitting a while with Him that day, thought
and over the days ahead returned, and
leaving only for food, drink and service
that Gautama would not be distracted
from His goal, until, upon returning,
he saw Him glowing in the morning light
and so began to dance with Him beneath
the tree. A leaf was shed, was gathered then
and the boy, who while tucking it away,
Gautama asked if he would run for Him,
to village, crossroads, field, grove, wherever
Gautama wished to speak. And so he ran,
and soon arriving, announcing thus His
coming— holding high the leaf he carried,
which had never died. Living— living and
green until Lord Buddha left His body.

Depths of Green (the second poem)

Depths of green— from canopy to forest floor
In streams of raucous livingness
And there, and where about, a sanctuary
Falls in heaps, in stone walls run aground.

And with, nearby, afar, by ins and outs
Through every place (perceived)
Wherever listened for— vibration.

A single voice in Pali— a single voice
Leaping, leading, dancing, sweeping.

Hello. You greet me.

And if I split myself (the third poem)

And if I split myself and stand
At every corner of said universe
On any selfsame summer day
With any selfsame afternoon rain
Will this, though thought— this slip
Where densities of interest fail
(*Or by failures to perceive*)

This leaf-boy-runner
Eight portions of beingness
The full and fill of prime creation

(*Perhaps where life has paused*
Or slowed enough to perceive
At any speed
The speed of perception
The true speed of light
The wavelengths of laughter
And of any thing)

While density shifts
Where inertia has failed

(*The density of my interest*
The shift of my affinity)

There is no doubt
It has velocity
It gives back light
It bends the universe
It has location
From which expands
All space
Not already filled
With the logic of otherness
And even there it bends to will

As (*my breadth of vision*)
A torrent
An avalanche
A fissure in nothingness
A co-creation of All
This theatre
Our audience
Of stelae
Beacons of lostness
To wander by
In search of wavelengths
Of affinity

Where you might
Where I have
The curves beneath our frequencies

The pitch and roll of their design
Their width

(*We have*
Each other)

In all that vastness
An ordinary leaf
From this
For that
(*I am*)
The breathless
Runner

Cool in the shade (the fourth poem)

Cool in the shade
still dancing
with Lord Buddha

My phone is silent

My phone is silent.
You have not called— still not called.
What else have I done?

Rise

My skull lies split in splintered bits,
My brains, upon the rocks.
I rise on warring winds
To War

In battle over battlements
Where saints and saviors trod.
I rise whole, a king no more,
Nor more, nor less, than gods.

Another

I think a thought
(I sometimes do),
I think a thought
from start to through.
And when I'm done,
if it was fun,
I think me up
another one.

Coming of Age

My feet sing
My heart sings
My body sings along

     I'm already in love
     Just gotta find me a girl

At the turning, soon the lifting, of the night

I dreamed an opened book of prayer
On a table by a window
Pages turning by a window's ledge at night
There, God in darkness, knowing, seeing
And where a thief had hidden, kneeling
As pages flutter with the curtain in the night

Pages lifting, lifting, turning
While God looking, quiet, waiting
For His thief in contemplation
Of the faith he had not kept
There, in the shadows of the curtain
At the turning, soon the lifting, of the night

Head bowed

Head bowed. Homeless.
What a heavy load
he carries.

You sit

You sit, you stand, you read
the news. How marvelous
that you do not weep.

Let us say

Let us say that we have loved and though good
women, though good men, admit the hatreds too.

And looking, just by looking, find that love may be the
greater of the pair and love the bed upon which hate
must heal.

Let us say that we have loved.

Cataclysm

they fucked us back / we fucked them down / on in
the air / in on the ground / millennia / millennia / we
carry on

from thundercloud / we fleet as rain / clapping
corrugated tin / rising from the sea again / rising
silently again

under dark assembled things / assembling /
assembling / broken straws / severed wings / in all
the ground a war of things / too late / we carry on

The Mathematics of the Shattered Soul

The mathematics of the shattered soul:
Faux theorems born of arithmetic chance
Associations purged of higher goals
Dreams of psych (and pharma) courtesans

Whilst mystery lies in algebraic shoals
False purposed ranks of prophets blindly dance
And madmen peddle poisons from their towers
Thus Man is kept in ignorance of Man

Enjoy the sunshine when she comes

Enjoy the sunshine when she comes
Enjoy the blue skies cleared of grey
And with a glad song in your heart
Enjoy the sunshine when she comes

Enjoy the sun through dancing leaves
Enjoy her warmth against your skin
Enjoy the flowers and the green
Whatever else your day may bring

Enjoy the sunshine when she comes
It's been a while my dear old friend
Since we have walked and talked and laughed
Something we should do again

Enjoy the sunshine when she comes
Until then—

One Cat, Maybe Two

Raymond shifted his weight forward on the coffee shop chair and leaned his cheekbone into the heel of his palm.

A childhood verse chided him in his mother's voice of over fifty years ago

> *"Raymond, Raymond, if you're able,*
> *get your elbows off the table.*
> *This is not a horse's stable*
> *but your mother's dining table."*

It didn't immediately connect to any pictures in his mind but he had heard it enough to know it was real.

An hour ago he had been at his mother's side in the palliative care ward. She had appeared smaller than he liked to think of her— had looked almost like he was seeing her at a distance.

She hadn't greeted him, only closed her eyes and said, "Feed the cats, will you?" It wasn't really a question. "Yes," he answered, but the cats, whoever they were, must have left or died years ago.

The only living thing she owned, he suspected, was the small Christmas Cactus someone had brought to cheer her up. He looked at her again, waiting for her eyes to open. They never did. Her jaw dropped and that was that.

Raymond hadn't wanted to be in the room when the nurses and orderly would come to take her away. He stopped at the reception desk to say that he'd be in the coffee shop waiting for his brother and sister-in-law to arrive. They were late and he was thankful to have a few minutes to himself.

From where he sat he faced the open entrance of the café. There was a couple sitting tiredly off to one side. A man in a shapeless blue hospital gown and slippers shuffled in pushing an IV pole ahead of him. Raymond heard steps echo sharply down the hallway. Here they are, he thought, hurrying needlessly.

Bill and Marijke had been fast asleep at 2:30 am when Raymond's first text message came in. They never saw it until 5:30 when Bill reached for his cell phone as he did every morning right after Marijke turned off the alarm.

"Damn," he said, "No time."

Bill, "William" on his realtor business card, and Marijke, were used to demands on their time from potential home buyers. But they usually had early mornings to themselves—breakfast, coffee, catch up on current events. Not today. The text had said, "ASAP." They hit the drive-through at Starbucks on their way to the hospital.

"Hey Bill, Marijke," Raymond said. Bill nodded. "Hey," he replied and paused to look at Raymond to see if he'd say something else, "Is she gone?" "Couple of hours ago," Raymond said. "Should we see her?" Bill asked. "Can if you want, I suppose. Maybe later. Did she have a cat?" Raymond asked, "She mentioned cats. I haven't seen any for years. Did you take them?" Mother might have mixed him up with Bill again.

Raymond looked at his brother who didn't seem to be listening and then at Marijke. "She used to feed the neighborhood cats before she broke her hip," Marijke said. "That might be it." It seemed odd that Marijke knew more about his mother's life than her sons did.

"Maybe you're right," Raymond said. "What's next?"

"I'll call her lawyer and get him on it," Bill answered.

Raymond suddenly realized that his brother had been listening. Marijke started to cry. Raymond pulled some napkins from their holder and pressed them hard against his eyes. Bill looked down and away.

Over the next few days life seemed to stop. Nothing more than daily routines and only as long as they didn't require much effort or attention: coffee, whatever was in the fridge— dishes sat in the sink.

Gradually he began to feel alive again. It was as though he had been wrapped in blankets, hearing distant, mostly muffled voices, glimpsing unfamiliar rooms and spaces when he closed his eyes to sleep.

Marijke had startled him this morning when she called and said to the answering machine that they were coming over with something from the lawyer and hoped he would be in. She didn't wait for him to pick up. She'd have known he was at the kitchen table.

They arrived mid-afternoon. No knock at the door. Bill was the older of the two and was the most like their dad. And Dad had not been the knocking sort. Not with Raymond anyway. Bill and Marijke each carried a bag of groceries which they placed on the kitchen counter. "Thought you might need some things," Marijke said, "Nice to see you, Ray." She took a bag of groceries and made room in the fridge for its contents: milk, BBQ chicken and eggs. She placed the bananas in a wooden bowl.

"Saw the lawyer yesterday," Bill started. "He has the will but it doesn't amount to much except for the house," he paused. "The equity has mostly been sucked out of it. God knows what for. And there's this..." Bill dropped a large manila envelope in front of Raymond. "I've already opened it. There's an envelope for each of us in there. Marijke says we should open them together because we're all the family we have now." He tipped the envelope on its end and let the two smaller envelopes slip out. One each for William and Raymond.

Bill picked up his and tore the corner of the flap destroying most of the envelope in the process and extracted what appeared to be several sheets of neat handwriting. "It's just a letter," Bill said. He refolded the pages and put them into the inside breast pocket of his suit jacket.

Raymond waited a moment then picked up the other envelope, turned it over and nodded almost imperceptibly. He stood, walked to the shelf between the window and the back door where he had made room for the Christmas Cactus instead of leaving it behind. Not sure about the light, he thought, and leaned the unopened letter against the earthenware pot.

"Not you, too?" Marijke shook her head.

"It'll be like..." Raymond said, he paused, looking at her, "It'll be like not hanging up the phone." Marijke understood— he'd never open it. "I get it," she said in a softer tone. Bill looked blankly at his brother. And Raymond smiled a little for the first time in a while.

By six the next morning Raymond was already dressed and brewing coffee. Usually he would head down to Timmy's Donut Shop for his caffeine fix. "Double trouble," he'd say, meaning "Double double," as he always did at Timmy's. It amused him and often made his favorite server smile. "Too much trouble, you mean," she'd say.

Raymond guessed that some of the guys at the corner table would be wondering how he was doing. They'd know what had happened, of course, but they'd ask just the same.

He poured his first cup and walked out onto the back porch. Still a bit cool out here, he thought as he leaned against the railing, sipping his coffee as his eyes wandered around the yard. He'd have another cup in a while but first he had something he needed to do.

Raymond sat down on the porch steps and slipped his feet into an old pair of shoes. He tied them and flicked the loops with his finger to see how the laces fell, to make sure he had not tied them backwards and would not work their way loose. Someone had taught him that a long time ago when they had seen his laces come undone.

He stood up and walked across the yard to the back lane and the narrow picket fence, missing a picket here and there and much of its original coat of white paint. Some boys had probably pulled the missing pickets off decades ago and with galvanized garbage can lids for shields spent a Saturday morning sword fighting.

The gate was leaning and half open, held there by uncut grass, weeds and neglect. He stepped out and onto the lane that led between the two rows of houses that backed onto it. Raymond looked at each fence, each set of stairs and window as he passed them by.

A block later he turned and headed home satisfied that he had seen at least one cat, maybe two.

Another cup of coffee in hand, Raymond sat on the top step. On his way out of the kitchen and onto the porch he had stopped to turn the cactus in the morning light, stepped outside placing a saucer of fresh milk by the porch door, and sat down.

The New Apartheid

Yes, segregate.
Create a slum for me.
Build walls.

Render us apart.
Hide.

Paris, 13 November

I remember— I remember
The flying leaves and floating leaves
Blazing yellow-orange-red

Until, wind-felled, their final embers.
I remember to this day,
This wet wool-gray— this end of day

Paris, that November.

Them Birds That Cat

Yellow blue green white black—
they sit upon their perch
above the cat.

Cool cat—
she curls her tail and counts
and curls her tail,
she counts—
them birds.

That cat.

For I do love

For I do love
though love by step descends
through gates, along idyllic paths,
through grates and catacombs,
love ascends by love alone.

For I do love.
It is thus I am.
Amo. Sic ego sum.

Softly

Hold me, fold me
Like a dove
Kiss me now
Before I go
Here I am
Once more, My Love
My Love, before I go

Gently, softly
Like a prayer
Lay beside me
Hold me still
Defend me
When I fall, My Love
My Love, I fear to go

WAR

WAR is NOT a spiritual preference (except to the insane)
WAR is NOT a spiritual orientation (except to the Merchant of Chaos)
WAR is NOT a spiritual experience (except to those who die)

open our eyes together and we will dream
open our fists today and we will build
open our doors tonight and we will sing
open our eyes/fists/doors

(close your eyes and never mind
(close your fists and build collateral damage
(close your doors and scream

oh no
open our eyes/fists/doors

send our prayers to the front lines
send our light to the front lines
send our truth to the front lines
send us

and we will build for beauty

and for freedom
and for love

send us

Are we beggars

Are we beggars now? We beg—
We beg for peace. From whom?
The War-Men have no peace to give.

clatter

clatter fades
quiet
afternoon air

At least until this fairy tale is over

Her bags were packed, left by the door. She looked away waiting for her ride to come. Waiting.

You met her on a holiday. You can't recall who else was there. She's moved along and left you holding empty air. Empty rooms and empty halls fill the days you've lost count of and left an empty bed alone beside you.

You met her one late-summer day, or was it autumn, who can say? Like falling leaves you fell one with the other. The mornings were the best of all. The evenings melted into dawn and dawn again.

And then one day she said goodbye. Without a word, she said goodbye. Her eyes had someone else inside. You asked yourself when this all started.

Now every girl you see instead, and every time you turn your head, and all the names on every street, the colors of the sky at night, your bed at dawn, days pass you by, whatever tells you you're alive tells you that you're dead inside.

You keep her pillow by your own, wake up late each afternoon but still you wake up as alone. And then one day you've cleared your mind, you bring her back and let her slide away again.

Now mornings fade from grey to green, and somewhere in the days between you catch an eye, she catches you and spends a night or maybe two. The hallway and the living room, the shower and the kitchen floor, what else had they existed for?

Now every smell of every flower, every early morning shower and all the songs on every street, the colors of the sky at night, her kiss at dawn, the rising light, whatever tells you you're a man tells you you're alive again. Yet stories like this never end like fairy tales.

Every smell of every flower, every early morning shower, and all the songs on every street, the colors of the sky at night, her kiss at dawn, the rising light, whatever tells you you're a man tells you you're alive again at least until this fairy tale is over.

Embittered Immortal

Embittered Immortal
cries— Life's a bitch and you
never die— never die—

Hymn of the Fallen Tree

Let me rest among these giant souls that stand
where trees once stood.

Here, greens break into blacky-blues and dragonflies,
and dusts of beetle dung grow old withal.

Let me rest among the salmonberry and the
tumblewood of cotton, ash and hemlock, fir and
cedar.

And let the wind stir of pine above the fall reawaken
me in early greens and sapling dress, anon.

Sweet Home

When I am done with being right and you are done
with being wronged

Perhaps then we can speak of something small and
bright that we can both agree upon.

this-that

My home is in a sky
where night as clear as day
and only for the stars and us
and where I've met the dawn

I dream
to touch this-that, the sky again
the sweep of stars into the distant
slope of night

qui vive

unseen, sans wings
alone above an unknown wind

unsung, no throat swells
no tongue conveys, nor eyes contain

no flesh burns here
no doubt, no alibi

suns race silent far below
planets swing, comets chase

qui vive? la liberté
qui vive? freedom

I looked up and saw a star

I looked up and saw a star. And then another. I traced the light of some small piece of rock or ice. It might have been space junk but could have been a satellite. No way to know for sure. The moon was over there.

Star blue sky

Waking, right eye first, along the pillow line,
through the dark, and where the curtains part—
for a moment, clarity— a star blue sky.

Do not the mothers and the fathers

Do not the mothers and the fathers
of Islam love their daughters, love
their sons, love the children as ye love?

Pannin' fer Rhymes (an old miner's tale)

Well now— It was sometime in the spring of '49 just 'round Memorial Day in the Land O' Freedom... or so they call it. Anyways, I was sittin' up behind them hills... Y'know, nexta where God 'n' Hell musta had some sorta fuss or 'nother. Sorta desert. Sorta not. And I was pannin' fer rhymes— I kept comin' up dry— when alluvasudden straight outta the ground there's this tinklin', twinklin' musical sound. So I eyeballed the pan and gave it a twitch. Some verbs and an adjective peppered the dish. Good stuff, I s'pose. Fer a yarn they'd bin fine, but not fer perfessional-lookers-fer-rhymes. So I swished 'em a little and shook 'em again to see if that tinklin' mightn't be kin to the one that I found in the gully that night. It'd had to be good, or it wouldn't fit right. Them poets won't shell-out fer less than a pair cuz one by itself leaves 'em pullin' their hair. So ya gotta find more than a couple that fit or poets 'll fake it and some 'll just quit and some 'll just hope no one says that it's..... Y' know..... Call 'emselves "nou-veau" and claim it's legit. 'Nuffa that, I s'pose.

I looks fer them twinklin' musical words that rhymes like the first time they's ever been heard. I sure ain't the first one that's panned in them hills. My pappy before me turned up a few thrills and somewhere or 'nother done found a whole line. But me, I ain't happy unless it'll rhyme. They're there, I can hear them— they tickle the breeze! I'll stick it out long as there's poets to please.

If y' expected a yarn, or to hear miners cuss— I's pannin' fer rhymes and not them in the dust!

Hmph, what's that ya got there?

4 turtles lounging

4 turtles lounging
      as above so below
      numbers 5 and 6

Toss me high

Friends, do not hold me,
Toss me high!
Free to rise above the winds,
Above the darkness
Sadness brings.

Friends, do not hold me,
Toss me high!
Sing your Hellos!
And if we must,
A kiss goodbye.
Sing your Hellos!
And if we must,
For just a little while,
Goodbye.

Sixteen

You were sixteen and sweeter than a mountain spring when I met you. I was young and handsome then and love was bright and new. We were not old but old enough, and richer— more than all the worlds combined.

Come What May

Holding, come what may, each other
until unseen time folds us under

And if, and though by plan or chance, we pass
from out this life into another, yet another—
two parts within this Great Adventure

For us, for now, an hour more, a day, a breath,
no matter, come what may.

Afternoon

It was the early afternoon of Infinity when we met.
I had called into being the forever of time
to anticipate your arrival in finite rhythms
knowing they must be the whitest of lies.

The preparation, the perception, the recognition,
the intertwining and engagement of spaces,
their separations— all in the span of hello
and the impossibility of absolute goodbye.

Death of a Patriot

All that rest are spaces (space)
space of drums
("Come" they told him)

Nitre, cannon, horns, pipes
(echoed, calling)
vertebrae, rope-fray

Sinew (pink, foam-flecked)
flailing, fallen, gathered, apart
upon itself, weltered

The Meanings of Trees

pine is for leaving
oak is for time
willow, for grieving
love left behind

Incandescent

I have fallen while the stars of endless endless sucking skies have sucked me down.

Here, I have lain broken on the burning lawns of Hell—fingers, arms, soul— stretched to the points of no return to catch a wind that sings and does not sigh with the souls of a million million soulless men.

I have slept and dreamt of rising. Dreamt the cool nakedness of space beyond the shell of light that sucks me down.

And I have spent my fists with the soulless men against the blackened skies of Earth and the blazing incandescent trails of souls arriving— falling no further.

To dream this night of rising and the cool nakedness of space once more.

Pangaea

Standing. Alone.
A yellow sky. A shudder, grind
And hesitation of the earth.
Below, black seas heave and sigh
Against a scar of land.
Night. Yellow sky remains.
Arc and flicker.
I breathe. Night fades.
A shallow breath.
Acid rain falls gently.

Letter to the White Imbongi

These are the thoughts of the Locust thrum—

From the ripple, the thought is the Rock is God.
From the Rock, the Earth.
From the Earth, Sun-Moon.
From They the thought is the Milky Spiral,
The spiral known as the Eye of God.
And from the Eye all space is His
Gift of glorious and of noble heights.
And from the Eye all space is Hers.

These are the thoughts of the Locust thrum—

Praise them then— the Locust mind,
The flights of Stone, all Earths, their Suns
And every Moon. Praise Galaxies, praise Space—
Her heights!

These are the thoughts of the Locust thrum.
That which is done. That which is done.

White Seabirds Wheeling

Shoulders rolling, rising
as icebergs from their glacier calf to sea—
as men, we fend the rimless wilds

With force, flung, withheld,
intelligence, ancestral songs of origin,
of prophesy, returning avatars

Overhead
white seabirds
wheeling

Zombies

I see zombies in my headlights—
Just one or two— and now a few.

They come dancing from the darkness.
They fly twirling out of view.

Salty

Salty chips
Creamy dips
Licky lips

Ball Card Heroes

With bat and ball and gloves in hand and on our way
we'd pass by Old Man Finch where, when he'd sit and
watch the world, one of us would wave. Most times
he'd look, he'd say— Ever tell you boys about the
game?

He stole our breath away, sure, a hundred times. We
were fielders for him, basemen, catchers and every
ball split seconds from extra innings in mid-flight-
from-outfield-to-second-base-and-home-plate night
games.

Peanuts, beer, hotdog vendors shouting, with every
other voice, shouting! Out! You buncha losers! C'mon
c'mon c'mon! Safe!

Allow the call or fault it, either way. We were ball card
heroes, just the same, with bat and ball and gloves in
hand and on our way.

Orange Grove

If in some other life
we sat in endless space
(perhaps you came alone)
leaning in, could it have been
an orange grove?

If in another life
we listened (in this or
that other grove) and wept
and overflowed with hope—
Then it was real.

Glossary & Notes

Anon— [*Hymn of the Fallen Tree*] Soon.

An old word but I ask you, wouldn't a tree know and use the old words?

Cataclysm— [*Cataclysm*] A violent upheaval in the social order, in this case a series of upheavals across space and over millennia.

If life over such spans of time and space is unreal for you perhaps the idea of eternal struggle between good and evil will serve.

Calf— [*White Seabirds Wheeling*] A piece of an iceberg or a glacier that breaks away or the action of this happening.

Contrariwise— [*If (when)*] Introducing a contrasting condition.

Cotton— [*Hymn of the Fallen Tree*] Cottonwood.

e's— [*3201 e's*] The approximate number of letter e's in this manuscript. A reflection on the creation of poetry.

Fend— [*White Seabirds Wheeling*] To defend or attack with skill, make one's way. (Figurative)

Gautama— [*Boy Runner*] Siddhārtha Gautama, Lord Buddha.

Imbongi— [*Letter to the White Imbongi*] In South African tradition the name-title of a Praise Poet. The imbongi's art is in the composing and voicing of poems praising etc. a deity, a chief, a figurehead or other important person— Praises for what they have done, are doing or will surely do and the events surrounding them

I imagine a great imbongi with izimbongi (from the Zulu plural of imbongi) and other friends who relay information to him from far away. In particular, this poet writes about the thoughts he supposes have come from a distant cloud of locusts.

L'chaim— [*If (when)*] In Hebrew, a toast, literally, "to life." Pronounced here: l*uh*-KHAH-yim

Nitre— [*Death of a Patriot*] Canadian/British spelling of niter, a naturally occurring mineral used as a component of gunpowder.

Pali— [*Depths of Green*] An ancient language of India.

Pangaea— [*Pangaea*] Or Pangea, a supercontinent existing about 330 million years ago and eventually breaking into two continental masses, Gondwana & Laurasia. Gondwana was made up of areas now Africa, most of Australia, India, South America & Antarctica. Laurasia, of North America, Greenland, Europe and Asia north of the Himalayas.

Qui vive— [*qui vive*] From French, a sentry's challenge similar to English "Who goes there?"

Salmonberry— [*Hymn of the Fallen Tree*] Salmon-coloured fruit of the raspberry family which commonly grows along the Pacific coast of North America.

Sans— [*qui vive*] A word stolen from the French around the 15th century. It means "without."

Stelae— [*And if I split myself and stand*] Pronounced stee-lee. Plural of stela. An upright stone marker or gravestone.

Weltered— [*Death of a Patriot*] To lie soaked in blood.

Ye— [*Do not the mothers and the fathers*] Old word
for you

You can help.

Send anything from a comment to a complete review,
whatever you want to say, about a line, a verse, a
poem, anything that moves you from **3201 e's**— to
its amazon page or to poetkevinjtaylor@gmail.com.

Thank you for being here. Thank you for making this
worthwhile.

Love, Kevin

95916543R00046

Made in the USA
Lexington, KY
18 August 2018